PIANO DUET PLAY·ALONG
VOLUME 22

1 PIANO, 4 HANDS

RODGERS & HAMMERSTEIN

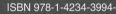

T0101576

ISBN 978-1-4234-3994-3

WILLIAMSON MUSIC®
A RODGERS AND HAMMERSTEIN COMPANY
www.williamsonmusic.com

EXCLUSIVELY DISTRIBUTED BY

HAL•LEONARD®
CORPORATION
7777 W. BLUEMOUND RD. P.O. BOX 13819 MILWAUKEE, WI 53213

Visit Hal Leonard Online at
www.halleonard.com

DO I LOVE YOU BECAUSE YOU'RE BEAUTIFUL?

from CINDERELLA

SECONDO

Lyrics by OSCAR HAMMERSTEIN II
Music by RICHARD RODGERS

Slowly, expressively

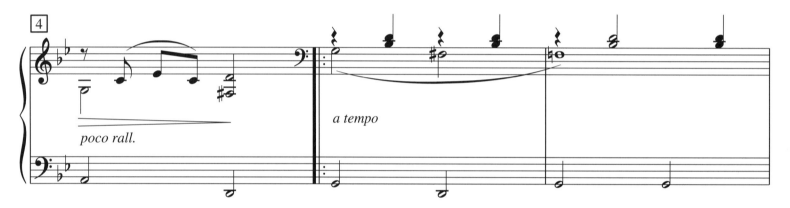

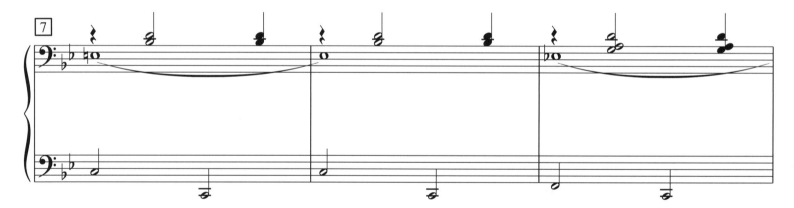

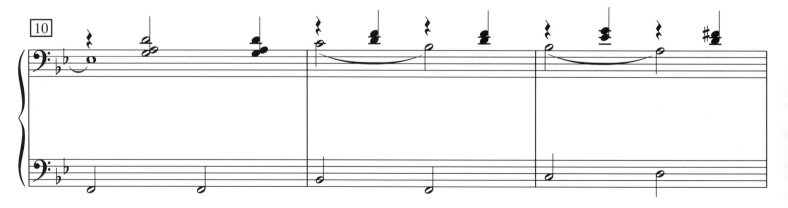

DO I LOVE YOU BECAUSE YOU'RE BEAUTIFUL?

from CINDERELLA

PRIMO

Lyrics by OSCAR HAMMERSTEIN II
Music by RICHARD RODGERS

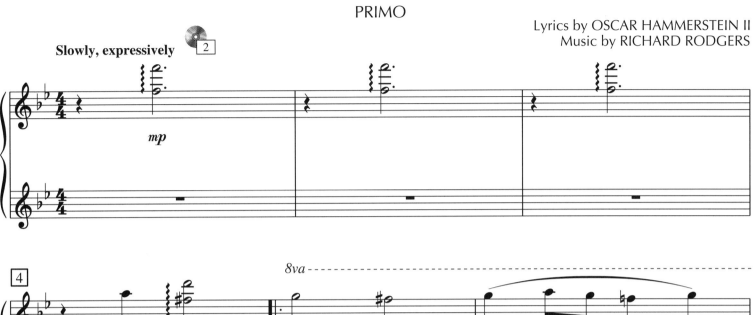

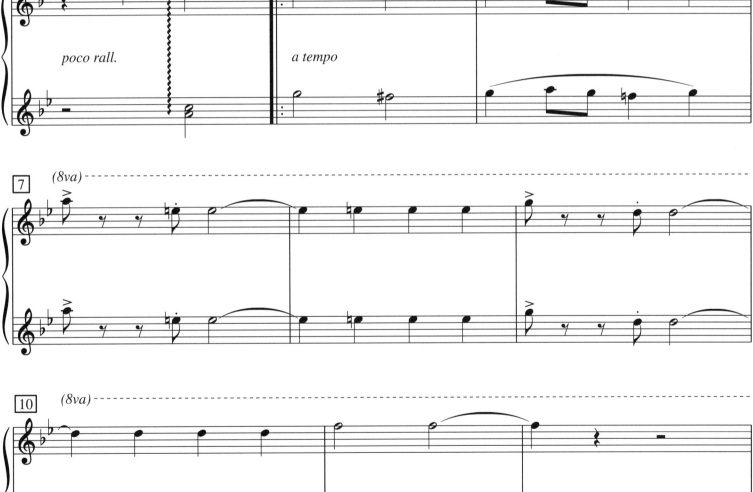

SECONDO

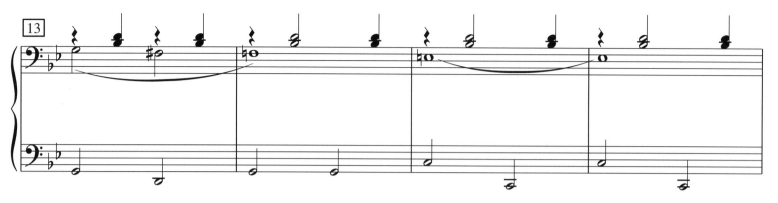

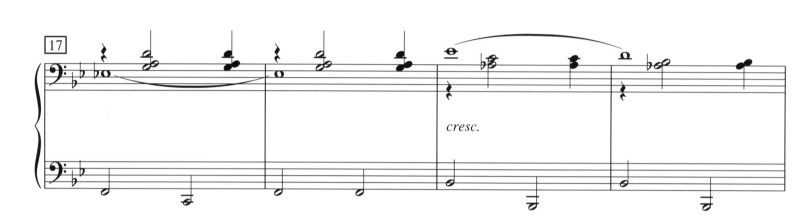

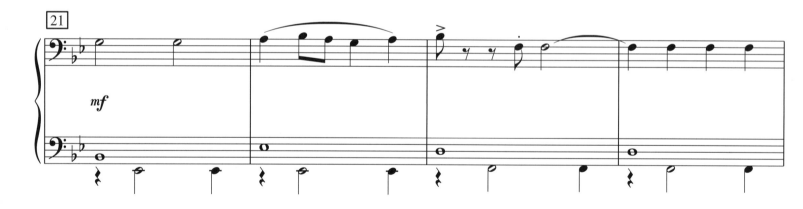

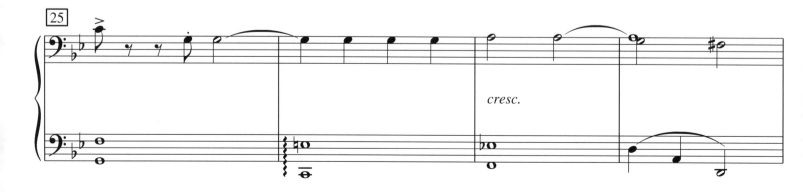

PRIMO

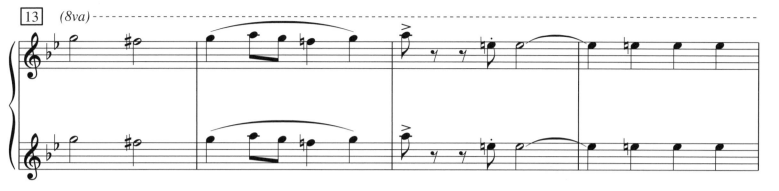

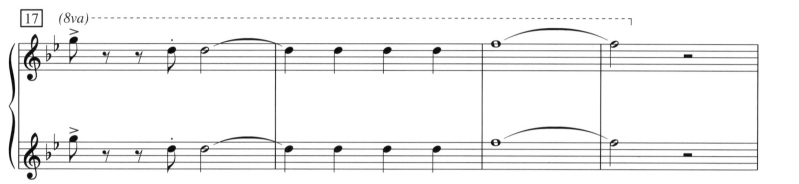

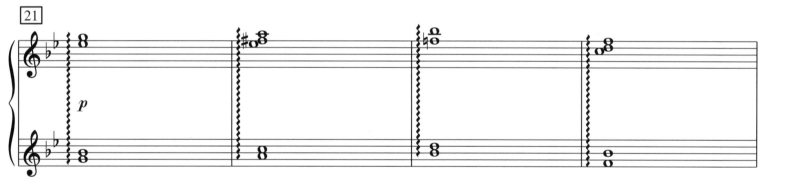

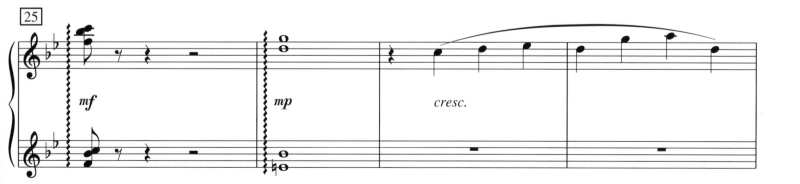

SECONDO

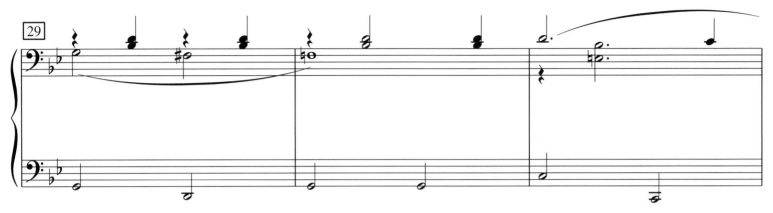

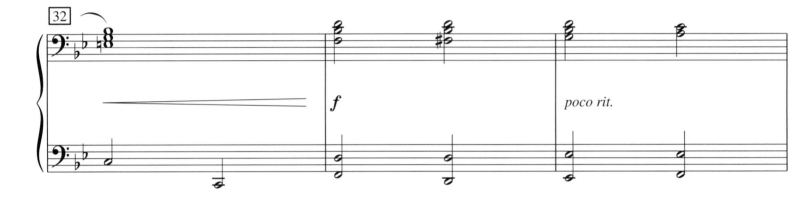

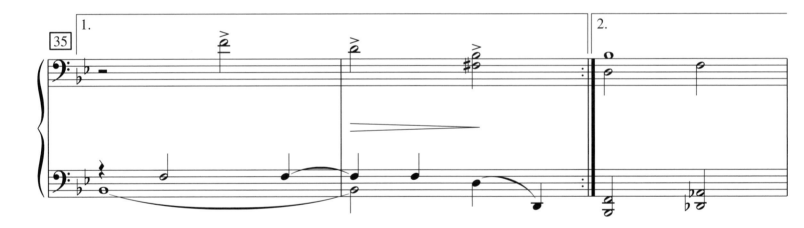

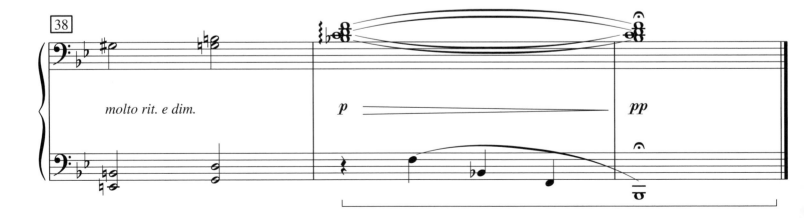

PRIMO

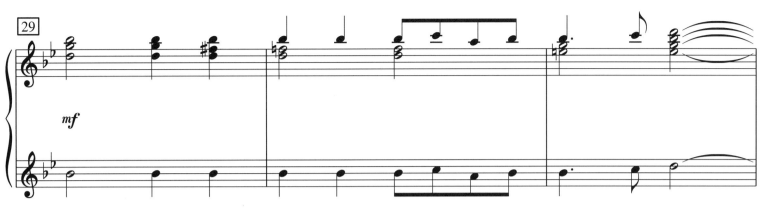

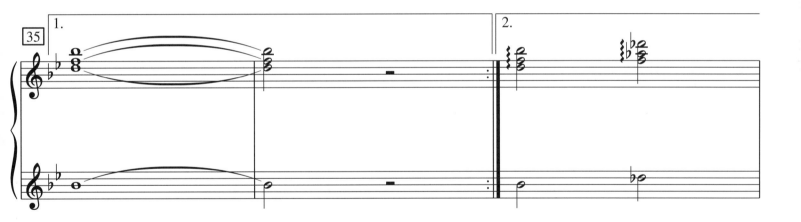

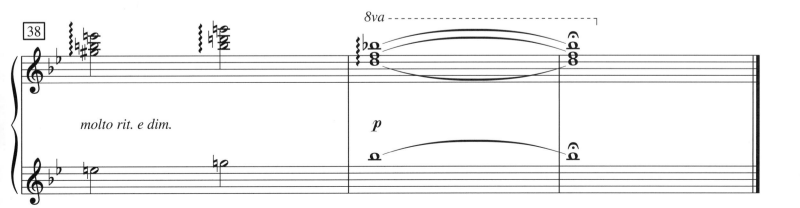

HAPPY TALK
from SOUTH PACIFIC

SECONDO

Lyrics by OSCAR HAMMERSTEIN II
Music by RICHARD RODGERS

Moderate, upbeat

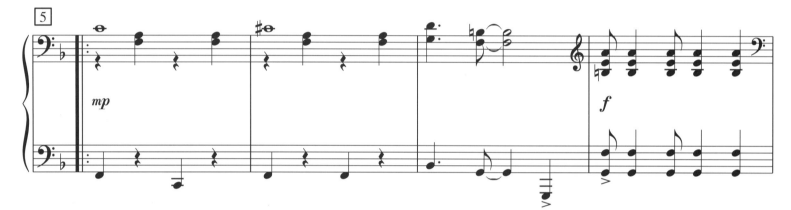

HAPPY TALK

from SOUTH PACIFIC

PRIMO

Lyrics by OSCAR HAMMERSTEIN II
Music by RICHARD RODGERS

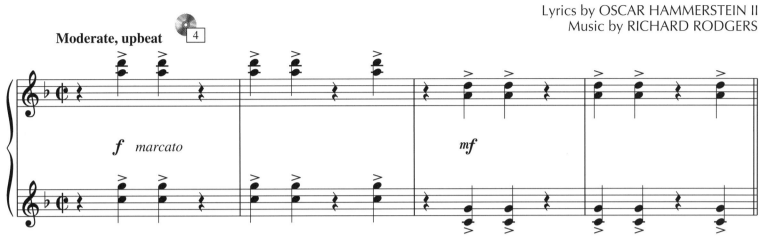

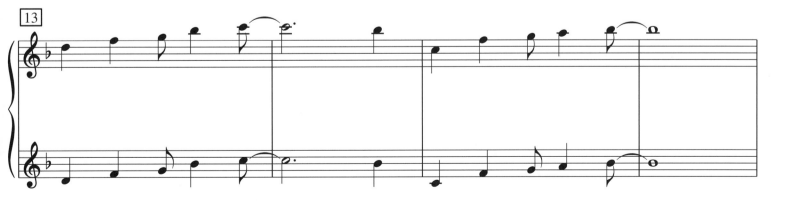

SECONDO

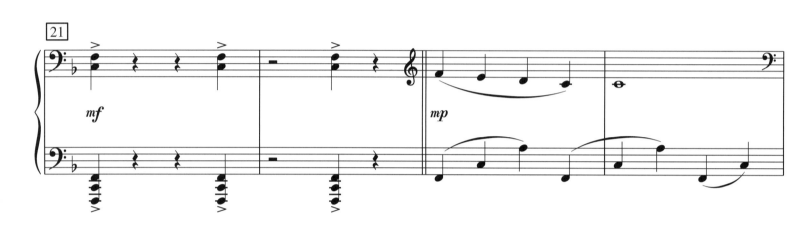

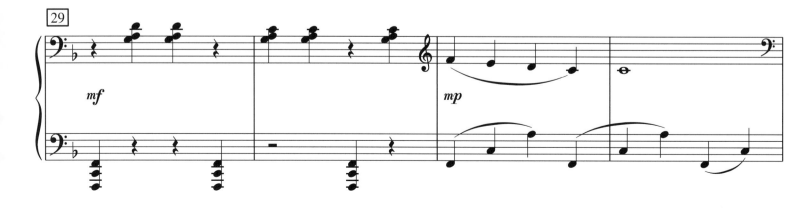

PRIMO

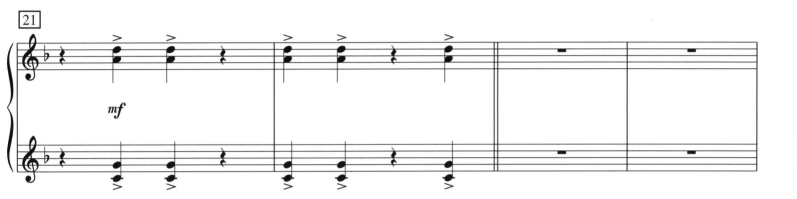

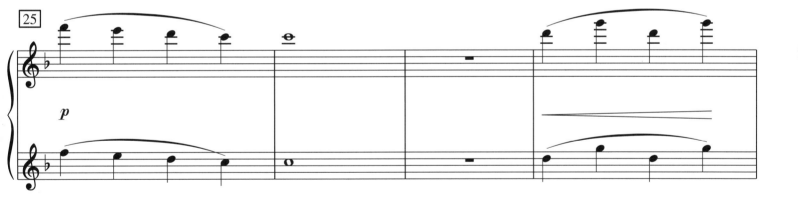

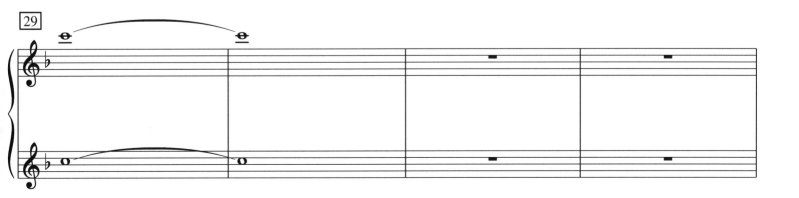

SECONDO

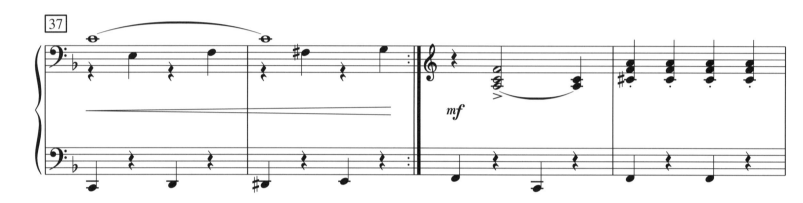

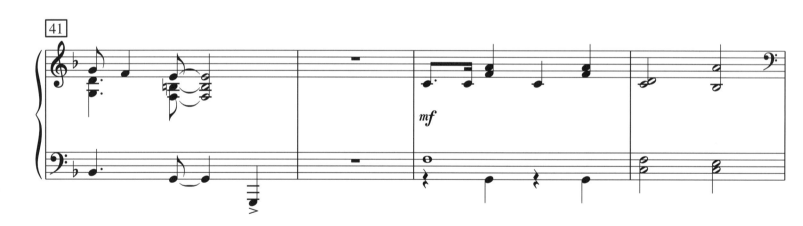

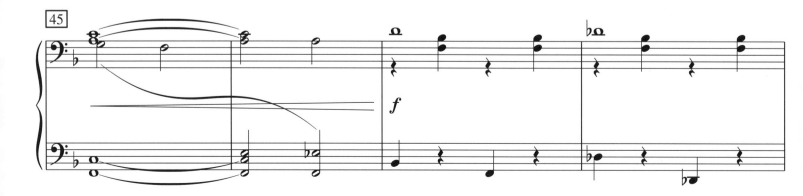

PRIMO

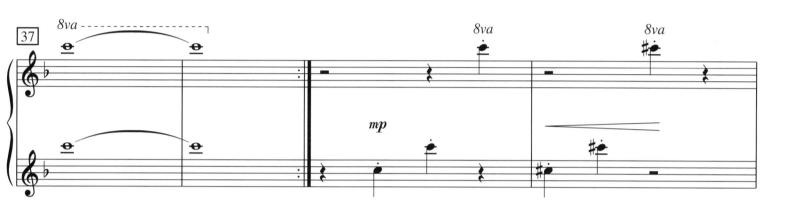

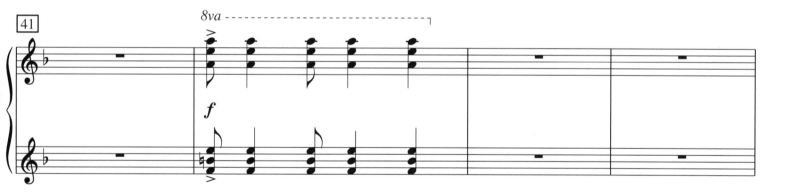

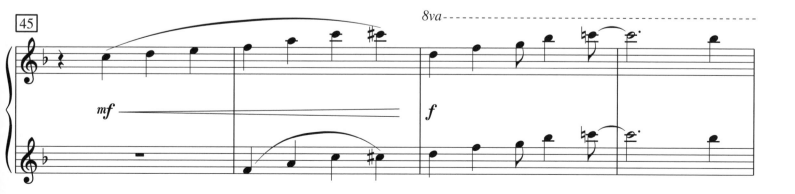

14

SECONDO

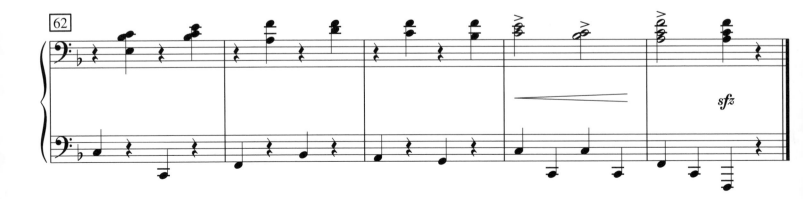

PRIMO

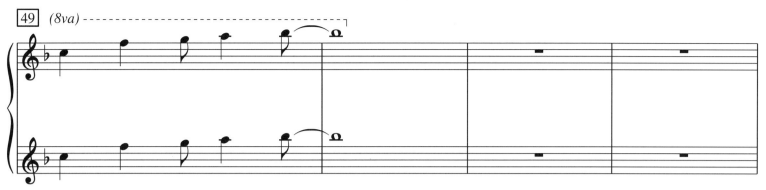

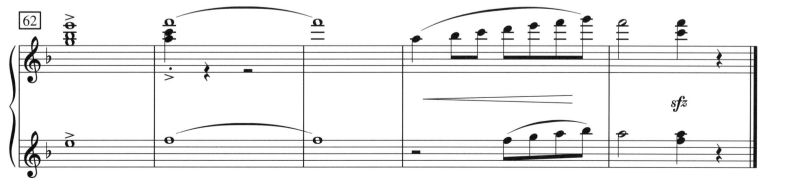

HELLO, YOUNG LOVERS

from THE KING AND I

SECONDO

Lyrics by OSCAR HAMMERSTEIN II
Music by RICHARD RODGERS

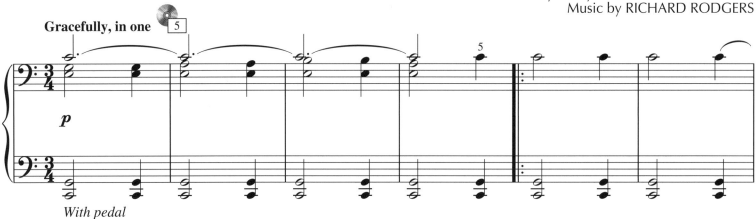

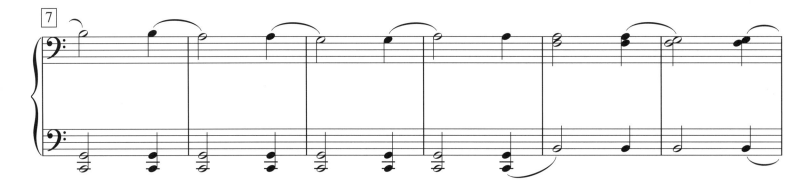

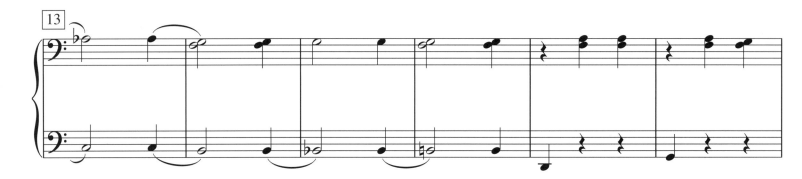

HELLO, YOUNG LOVERS

from THE KING AND I

PRIMO

Lyrics by OSCAR HAMMERSTEIN II
Music by RICHARD RODGERS

Gracefully, in one

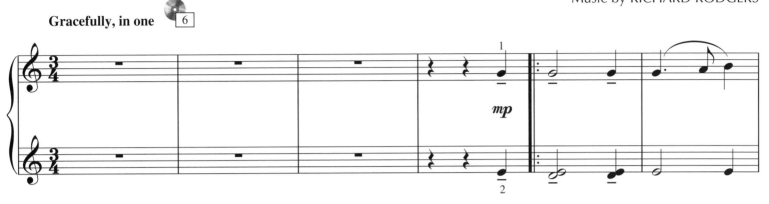

SECONDO

PRIMO

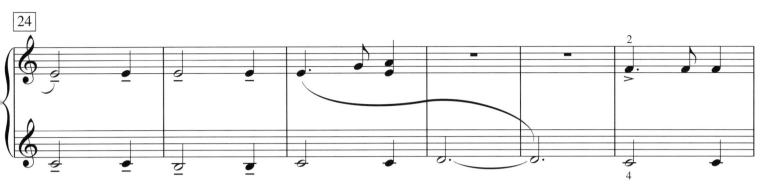

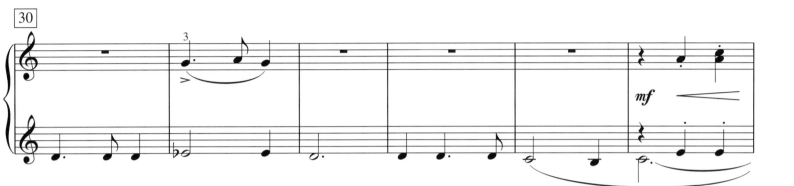

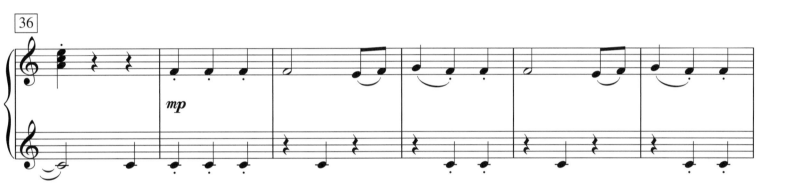

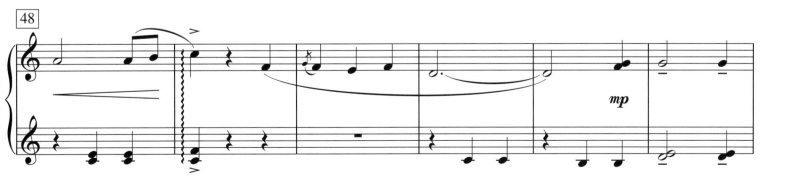

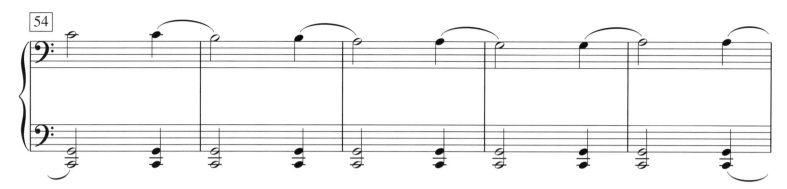

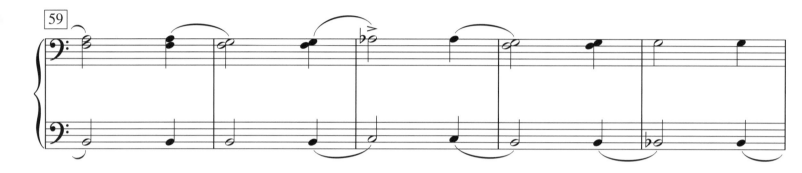

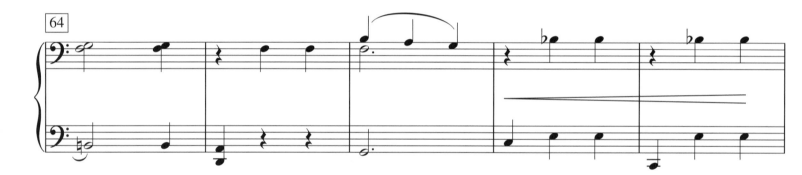

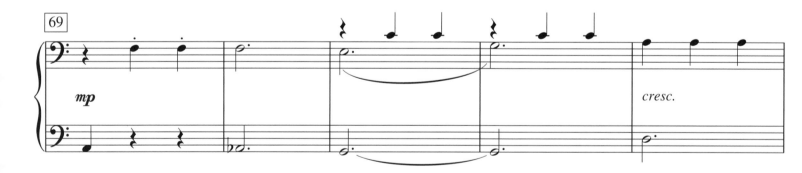

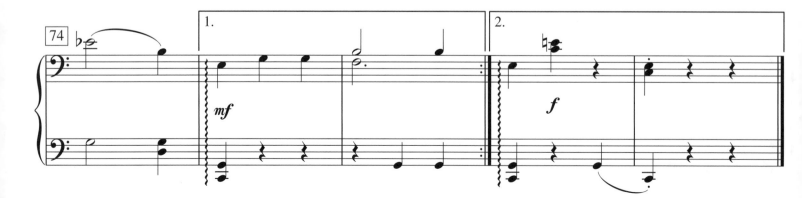

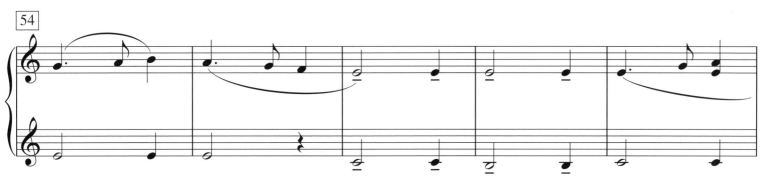

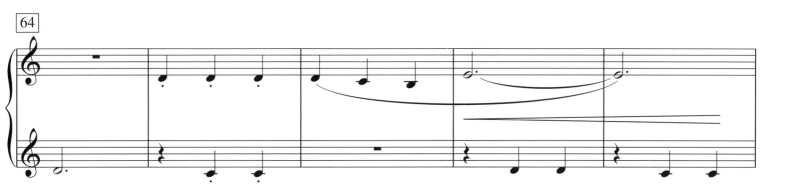

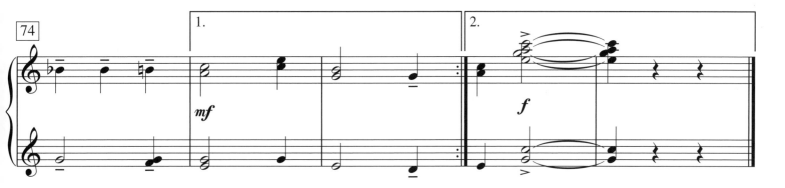

I WHISTLE A HAPPY TUNE

from THE KING AND I

SECONDO

Lyrics by OSCAR HAMMERSTEIN II
Music by RICHARD RODGERS

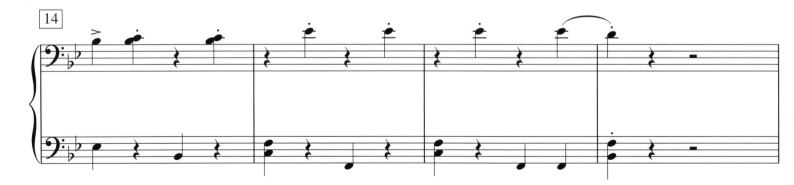

I WHISTLE A HAPPY TUNE

from THE KING AND I

PRIMO

Lyrics by OSCAR HAMMERSTEIN II
Music by RICHARD RODGERS

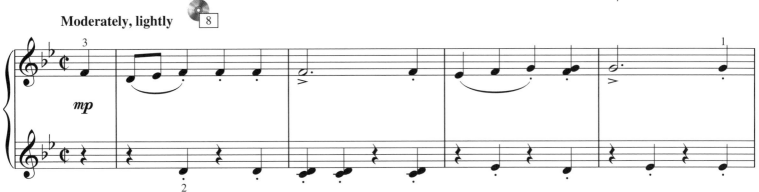

SECONDO

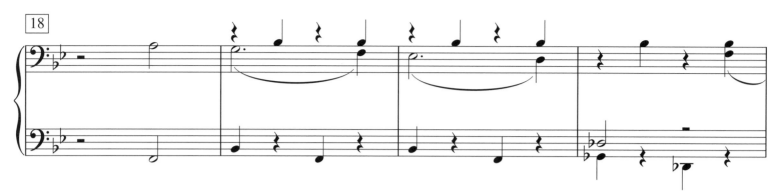

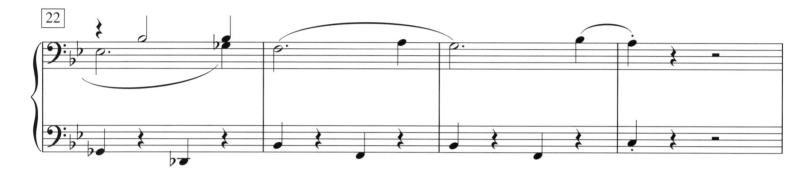

PRIMO

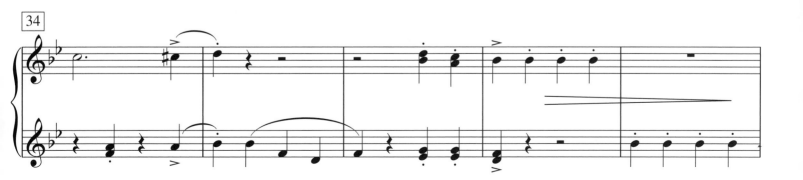

Coda

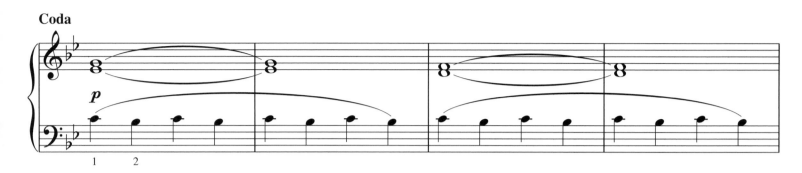

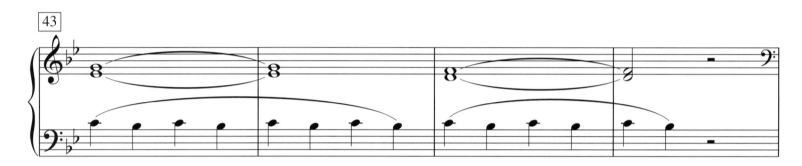

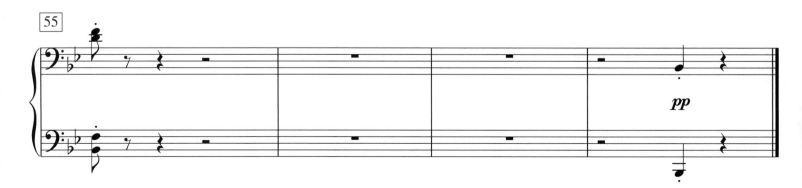

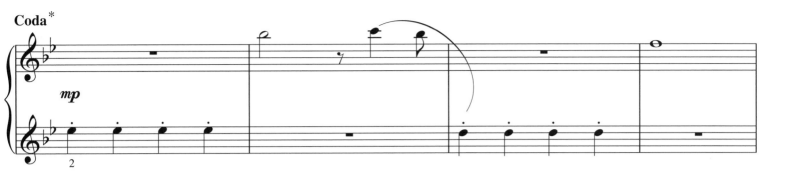

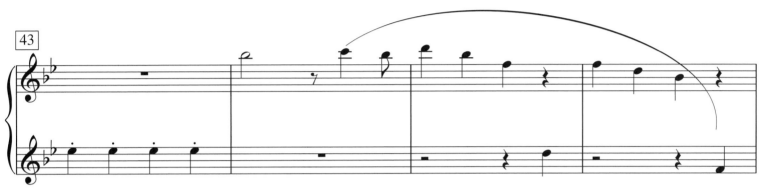

*The first eight measures of the **Coda** (Primo) may be played one octave higher in both hands.

IF I LOVED YOU

from CAROUSEL

SECONDO

Lyrics by OSCAR HAMMERSTEIN II
Music by RICHARD RODGERS

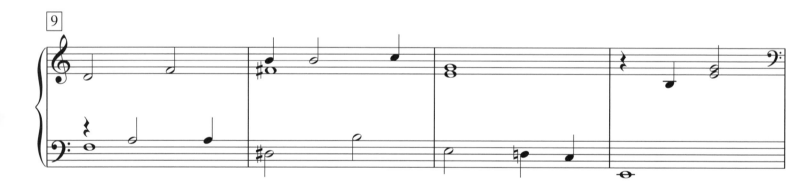

IF I LOVED YOU
from CAROUSEL

PRIMO

Lyrics by OSCAR HAMMERSTEIN II
Music by RICHARD RODGERS

Slowly, with warmth ($\quad$ = ca. 84)

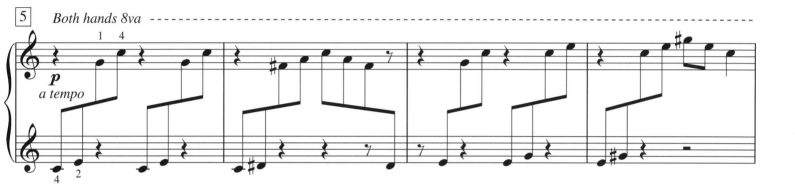

SECONDO

PRIMO

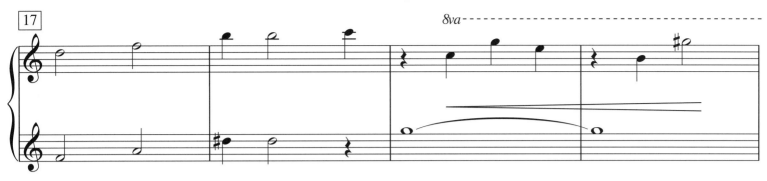

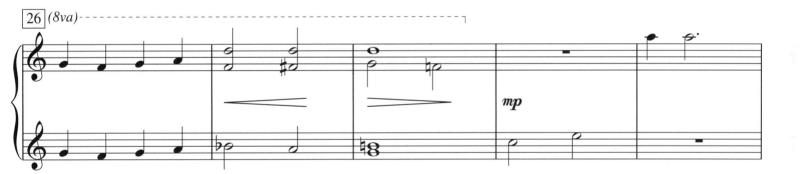

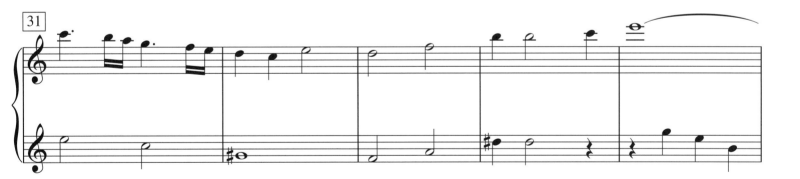

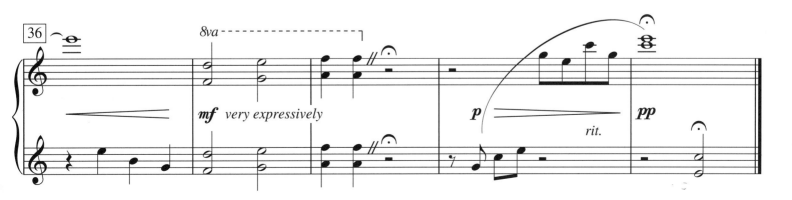

MY FAVORITE THINGS

from THE SOUND OF MUSIC

SECONDO

Lyrics by OSCAR HAMMERSTEIN II
Music by RICHARD RODGERS

Allegro (♩. = ca. 69)

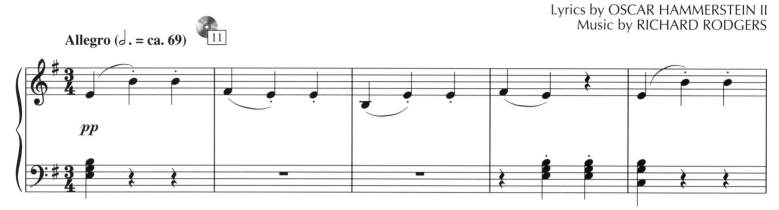

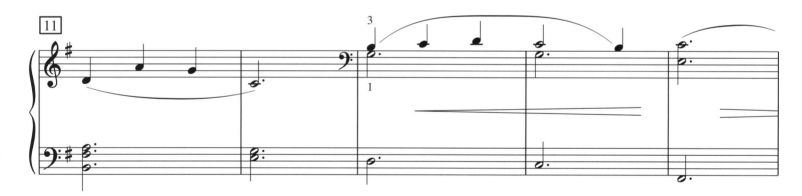

MY FAVORITE THINGS

from THE SOUND OF MUSIC

PRIMO

Lyrics by OSCAR HAMMERSTEIN II
Music by RICHARD RODGERS

Allegro (♩. = ca. 69)

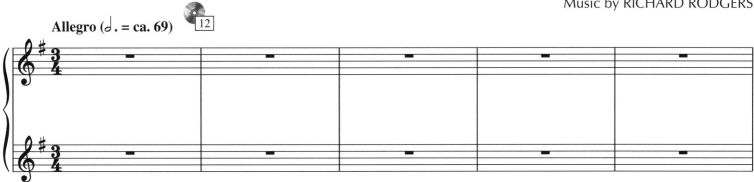

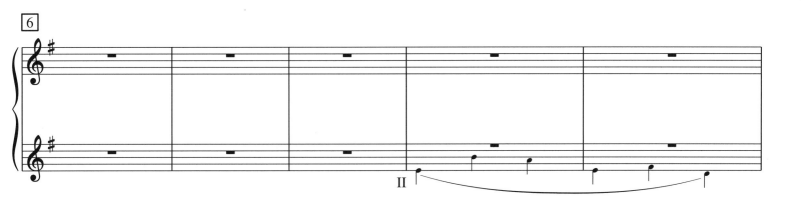

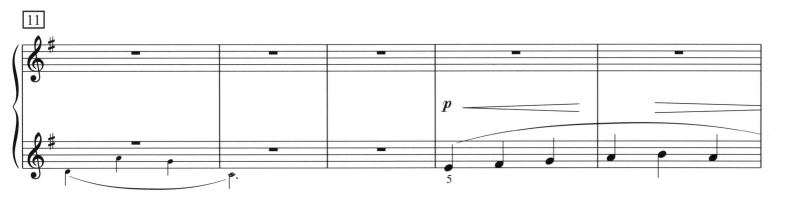

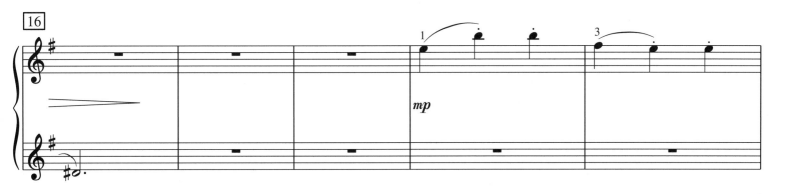

SECONDO

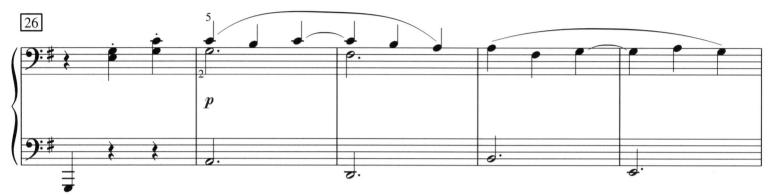

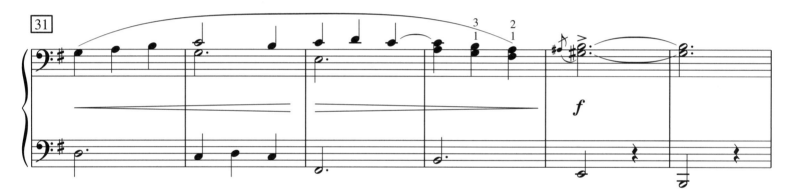

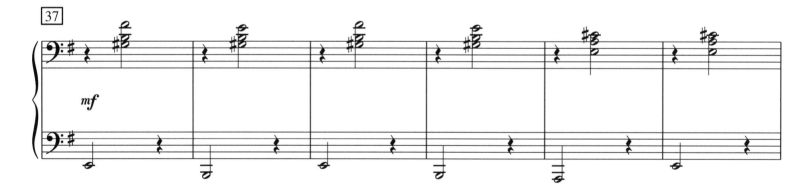

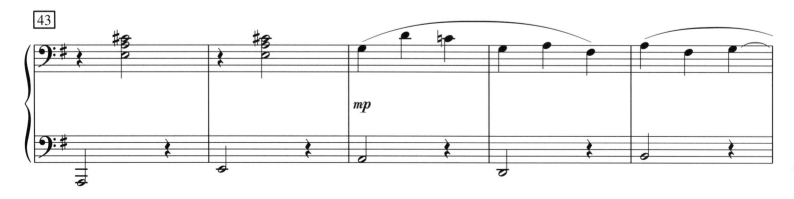

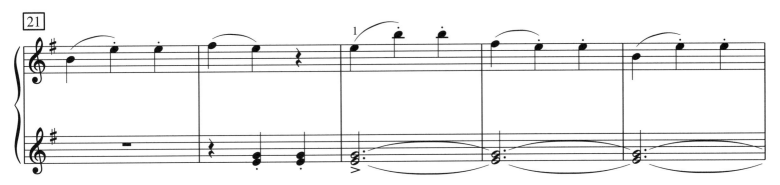

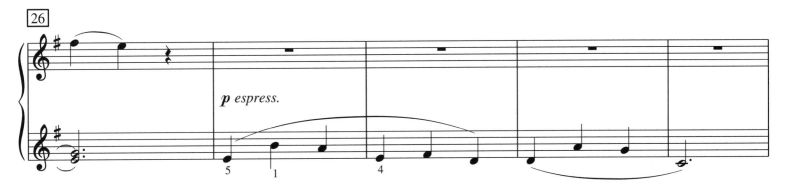

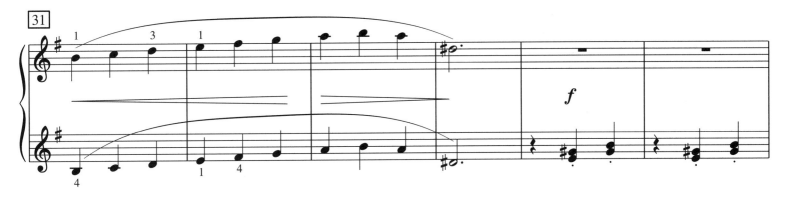

SECONDO

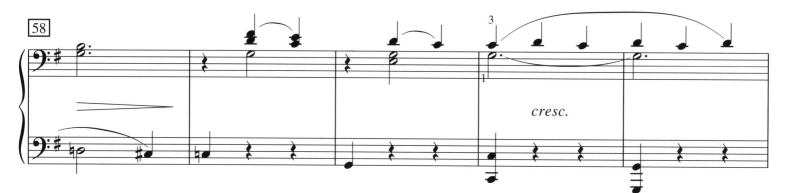

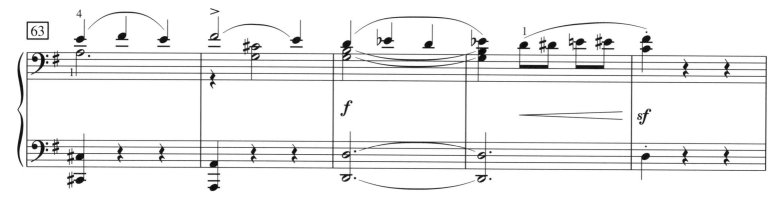

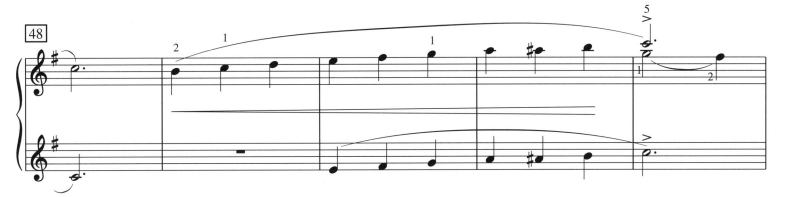

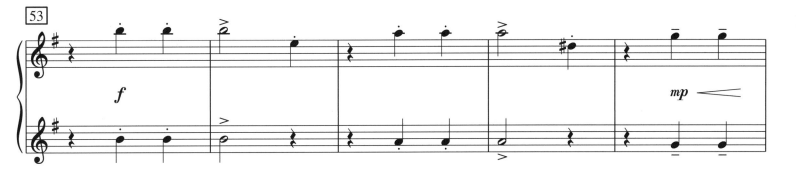

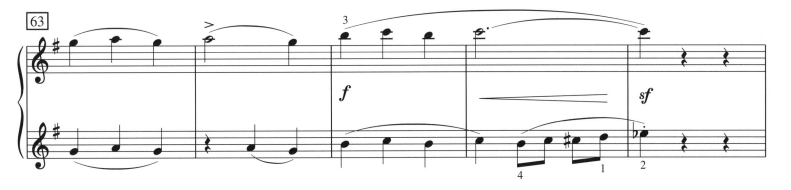

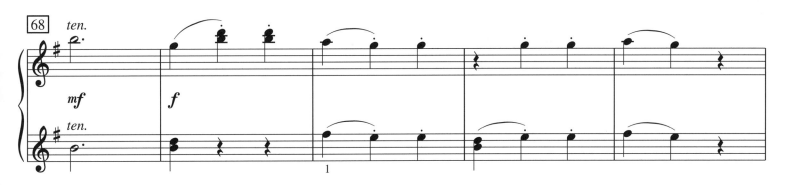

SECONDO

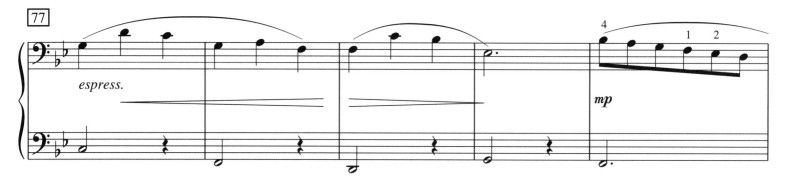

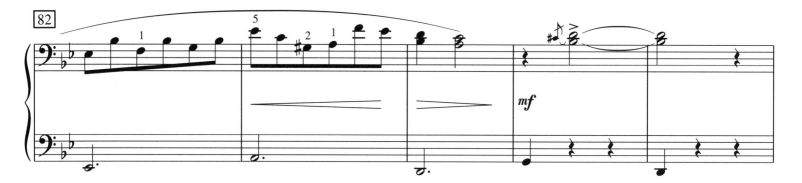

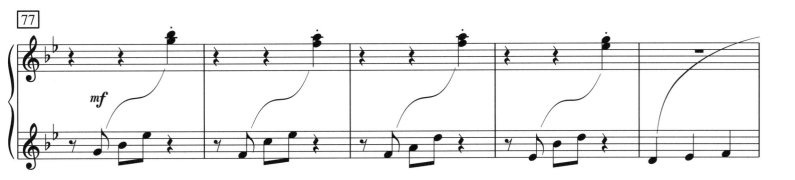

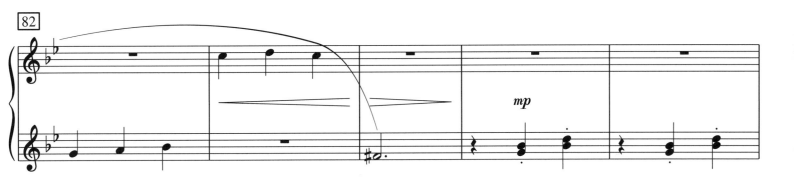

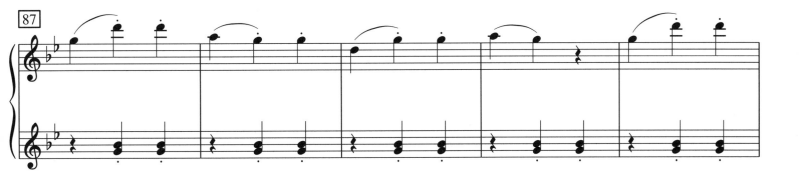

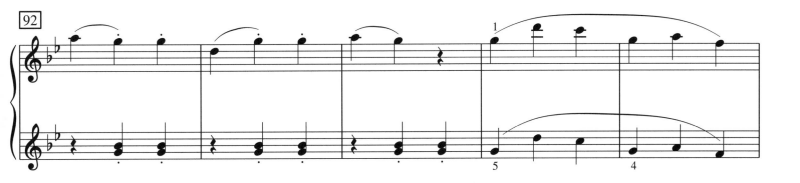

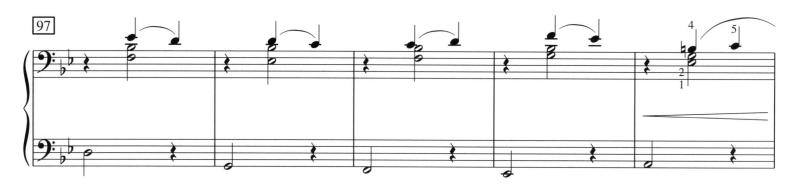

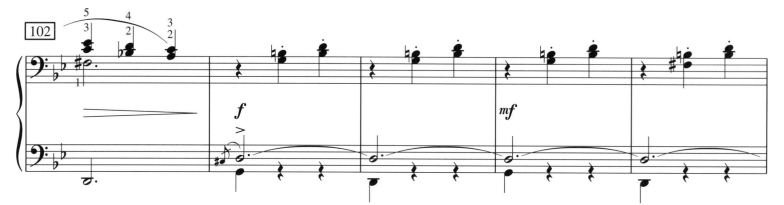

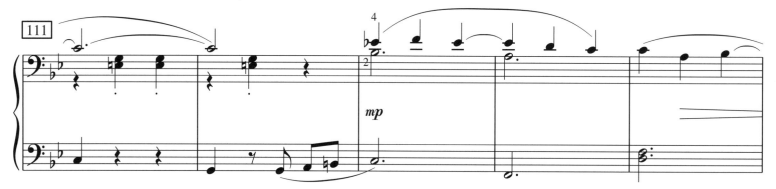

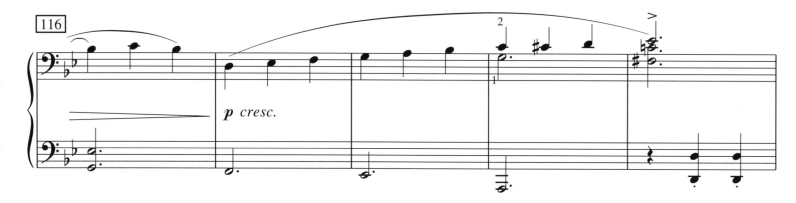

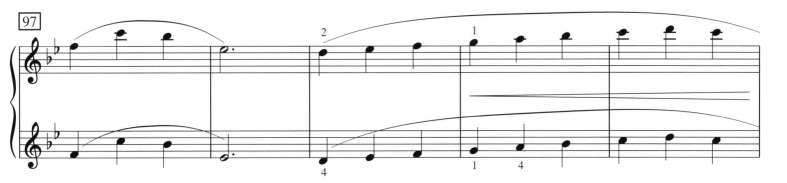

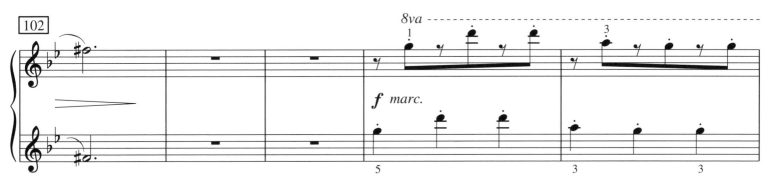

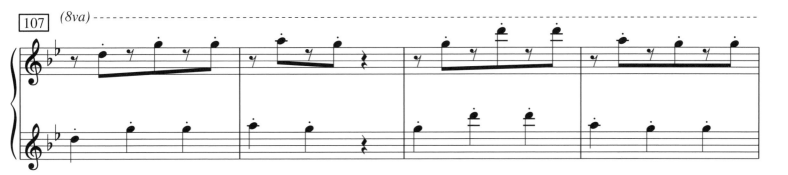

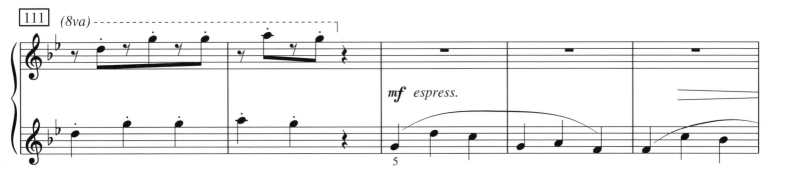

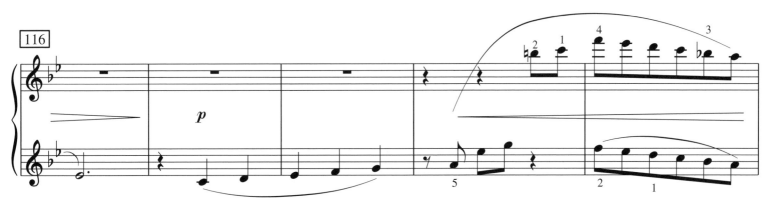

SECONDO

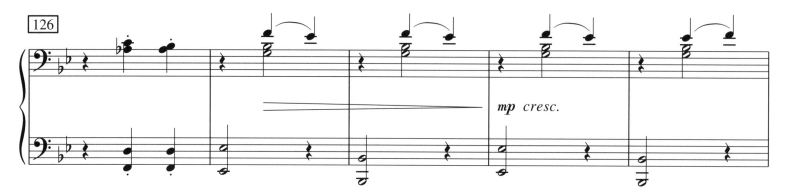

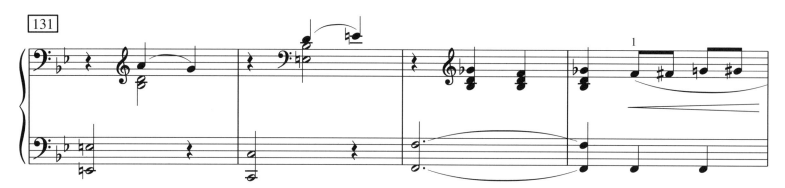

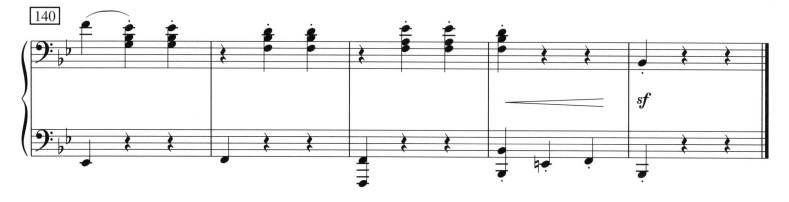

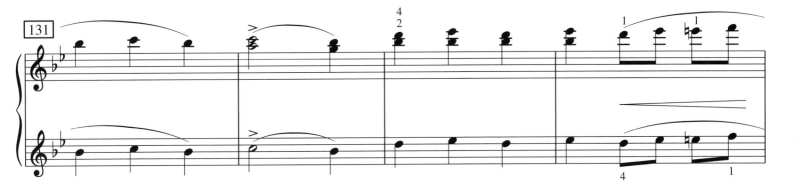

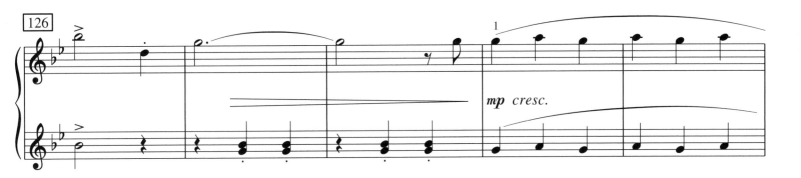

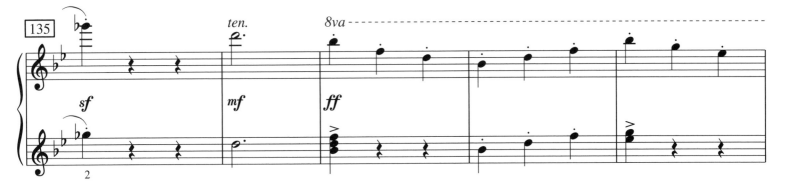

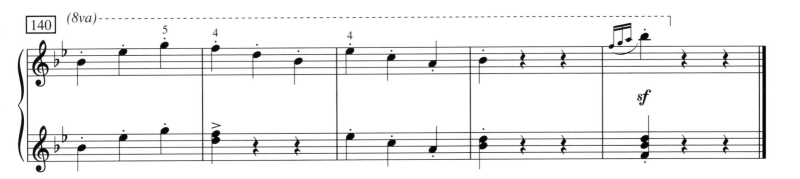

PEOPLE WILL SAY WE'RE IN LOVE
from OKLAHOMA!

SECONDO

Lyrics by OSCAR HAMMERSTEIN II
Music by RICHARD RODGERS

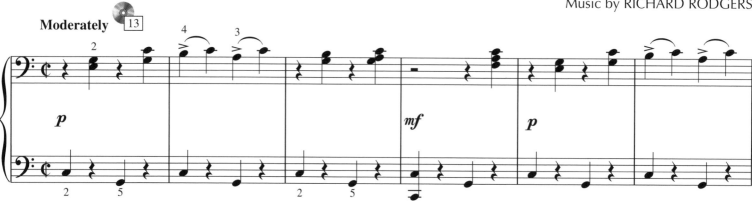

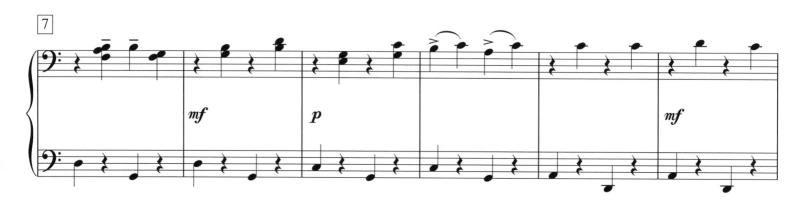

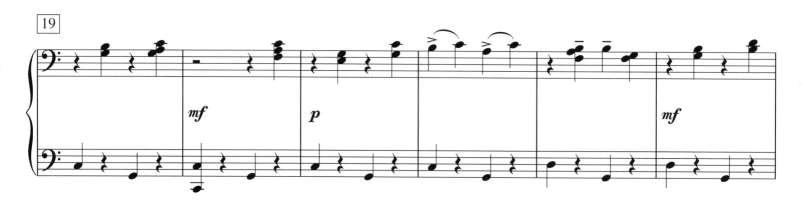

PEOPLE WILL SAY WE'RE IN LOVE
from OKLAHOMA!

PRIMO

Lyrics by OSCAR HAMMERSTEIN II
Music by RICHARD RODGERS

SECONDO

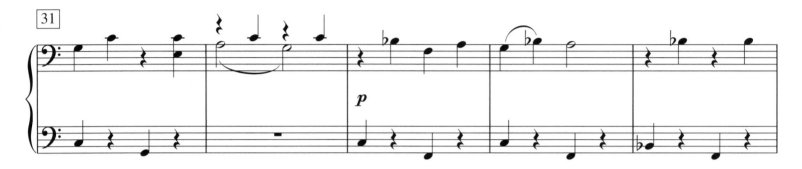

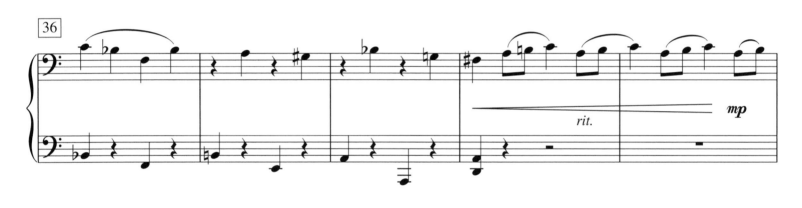

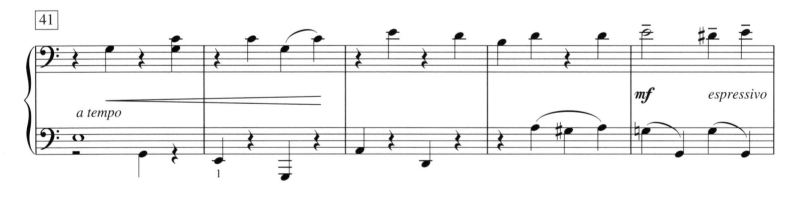

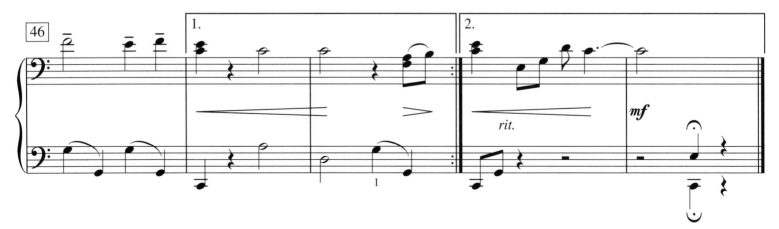

SOME ENCHANTED EVENING

from SOUTH PACIFIC

SECONDO

Lyrics by OSCAR HAMMERSTEIN II
Music by RICHARD RODGERS

SOME ENCHANTED EVENING

from SOUTH PACIFIC

PRIMO

Lyrics by OSCAR HAMMERSTEIN II
Music by RICHARD RODGERS

SECONDO

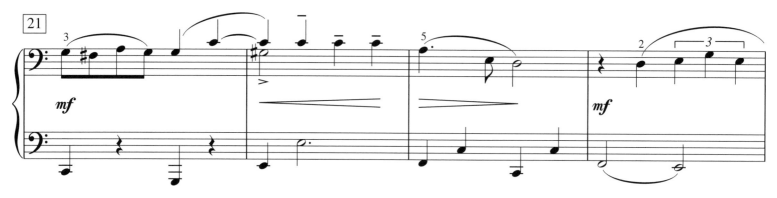

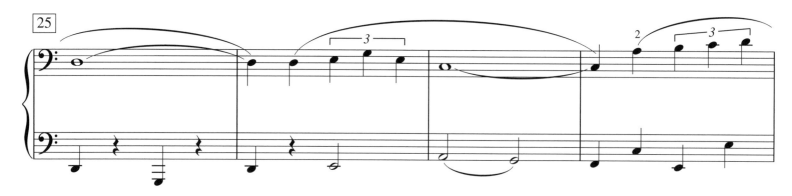

51

PRIMO

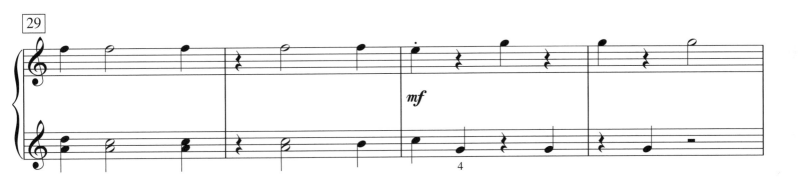

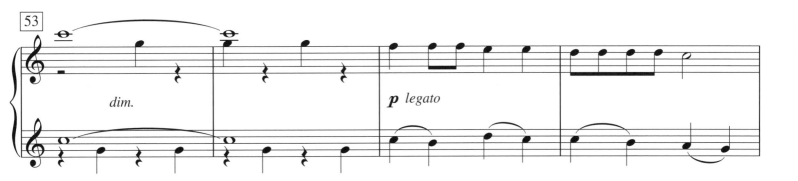

THE SURREY WITH THE FRINGE ON TOP

from OKLAHOMA!

SECONDO

Lyrics by OSCAR HAMMERSTEIN II
Music by RICHARD RODGERS

THE SURREY WITH THE FRINGE ON TOP

from OKLAHOMA!

PRIMO

Lyrics by OSCAR HAMMERSTEIN II
Music by RICHARD RODGERS

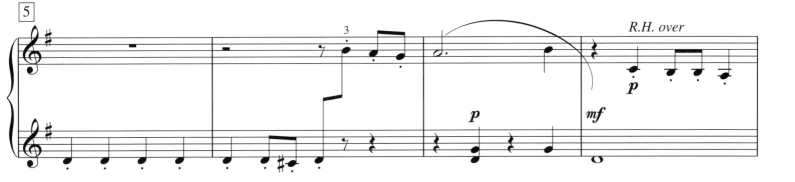

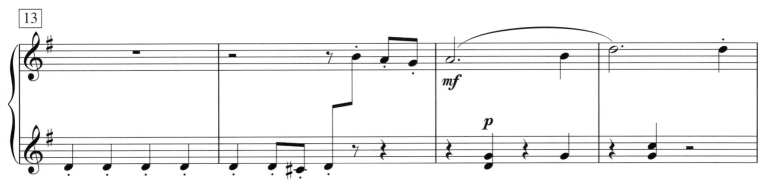

SECONDO

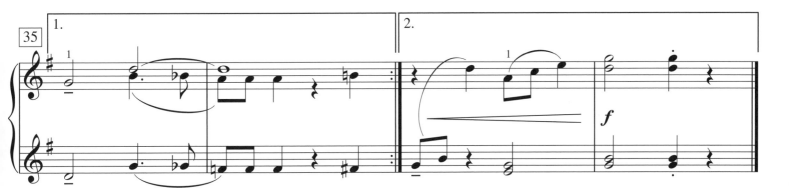

YOU'LL NEVER WALK ALONE
from CAROUSEL

SECONDO

Lyrics by OSCAR HAMMERSTEIN II
Music by RICHARD RODGERS

Moderately slow, with feeling

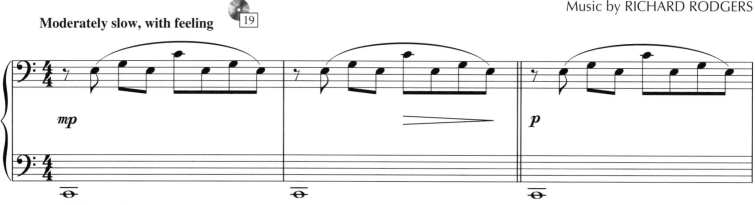

With pedal

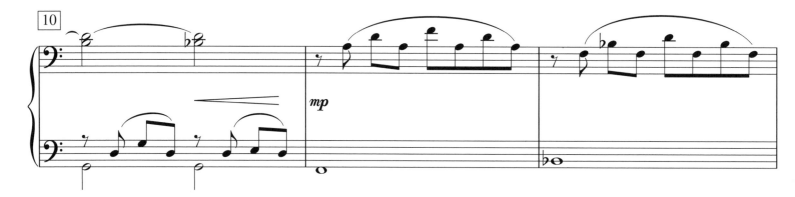

YOU'LL NEVER WALK ALONE
from CAROUSEL

PRIMO

Lyrics by OSCAR HAMMERSTEIN II
Music by RICHARD RODGERS

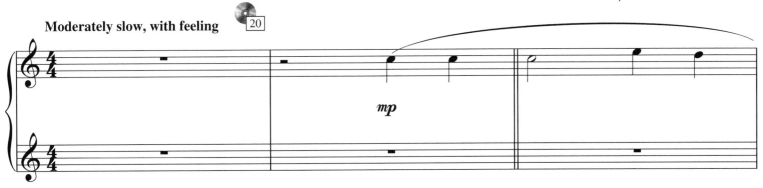

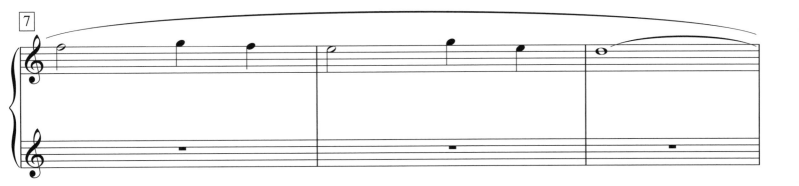

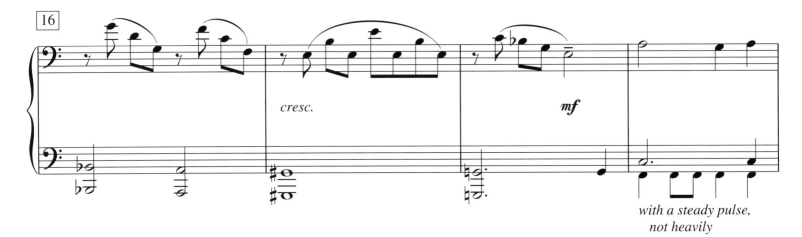

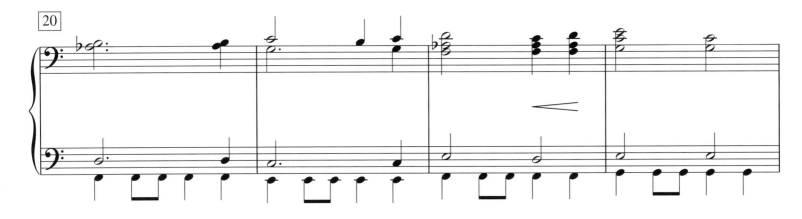

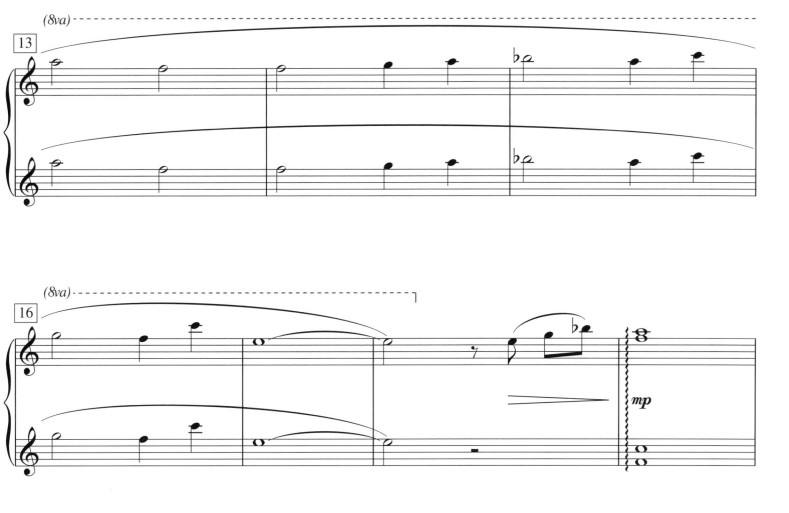

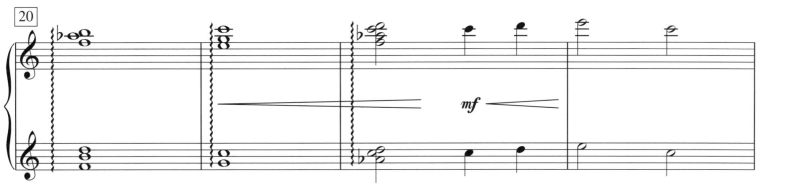

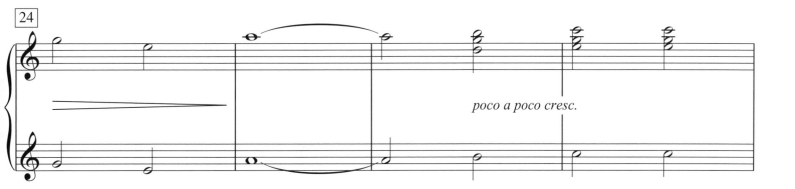

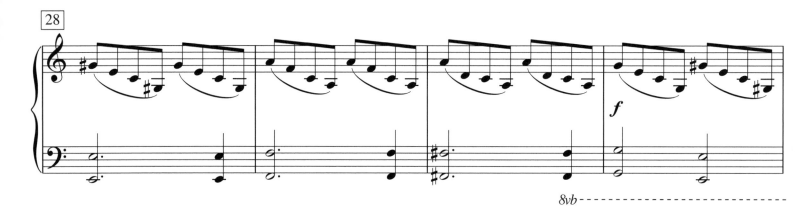

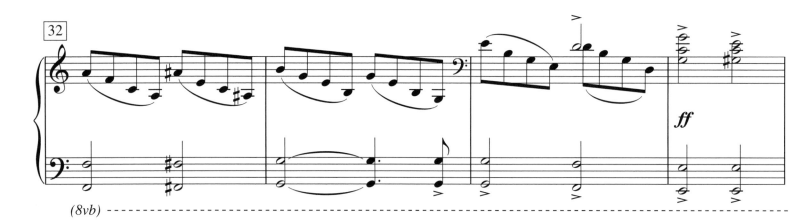

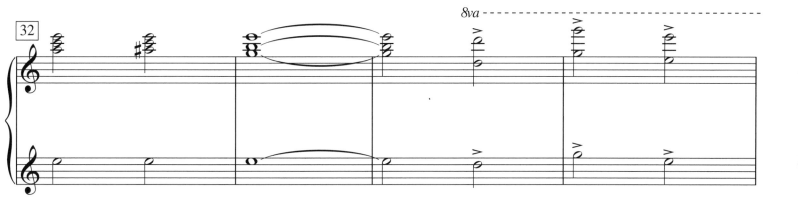

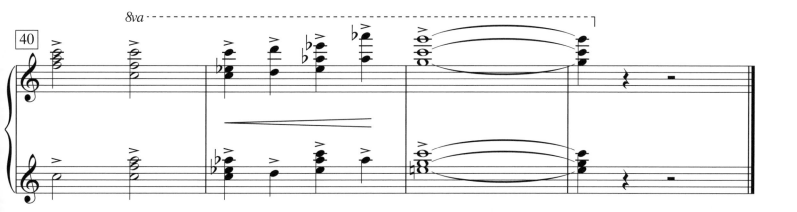

PIANO DUET PLAY-ALONG

The Piano Duet Play-Along series gives you the flexibility to rehearse or perform piano duets anytime, anywhere! Play these delightful tunes with a partner, or use the accompanying CDs to play along with either the Secondo or Primo part on your own. The audio CD is playable on any CD player, and also enhanced so PC and Mac users can adjust the recording to any tempo without changing pitch.

1. Piano Favorites
9 great duets: Candle in the Wind • Chopsticks • Don't Know Why • Edelweiss • Goodbye Yellow Brick Road • Heart and Soul • Let It Be • Linus and Lucy • Your Song.

00290546 Book/CD Pack $14.95

2. Movie Favorites
8 classics: Chariots of Fire • The Entertainer • Theme from Jurassic Park • My Father's Favorite • My Heart Will Go On (Love Theme from Titanic) • Somewhere in Time • Somewhere, My Love • Star Trek® the Motion Picture.

00290547 Book/CD Pack $14.95

3. Broadway for Two
10 songs from the stage: Any Dream Will Do • Blue Skies • Cabaret • Climb Ev'ry Mountain • If I Loved You • Oklahoma • Ol' Man River • On My Own • There's No Business Like Show Business • What'll I Do?

00290548 Book/CD Pack $14.95

4. The Music of Andrew Lloyd Webber™
10 great duets: Close Every Door • Everything's Alright • I Don't Know How to Love Him • Love Changes Everything • Memory • The Music of the Night • Pie Jesu • Superstar • Unexpected Song • With One Look.

00290549 Book/CD Pack $14.95

5. Disney Favorites
8 songs: Bibbidi-Bobbidi-Boo (The Magic Song) • Can You Feel the Love Tonight • A Dream Is a Wish Your Heart Makes • Hakuna Matata • Reflection • Someday • A Spoonful of Sugar • You've Got a Friend in Me.

00290550 Book/CD Pack $14.95

6. Disney Songs
7 duets: Candle on the Water • Colors of the Wind • Feed the Birds • Go the Distance • Kiss the Girl • You'll Be in My Heart (Pop Version) • Zip-A-Dee-Doo-Dah.

00290551 Book/CD Pack $14.95

7. Classical Music
9 classical favorites: Ave Maria (Schubert) • Canon in D (Pachelbel) • Dance of the Sugar Plum Fairy (Tchaikovsky) • Fingal's Cave Overture (Mendelssohn) • Funeral March of a Marionette (Gounod) • Humoresque (Dvořák) • Jesu, Joy of Man's Desiring (Bach) • Piano Concerto No. 21 in C Major (Mozart) • Sleeping Beauty Waltz (Tchaikovsky).

00290552 Book/CD Pack $14.95

8. Christmas Classics
10 holiday songs: Blue Christmas • The Chipmunk Song • The Christmas Song (Chestnuts Roasting on an Open Fire) • Christmas Time Is Here • I'll Be Home for Christmas • It's Beginning to Look Like Christmas • Mistletoe and Holly • Rockin' Around the Christmas Tree • Rudolph the Red-Nosed Reindeer • Silver Bells • and more.

00290554 Book/CD Pack $14.95

9. Hymns
10 sacred favorites: Abide with Me • Amazing Grace • Beautiful Savior • Crown Him with Many Crowns • Fairest Lord Jesus • Holy, Holy, Holy! Lord God Almighty • The Old Rugged Cross • Onward, Christian Soldiers • Rock of Ages • What a Friend We Have in Jesus.

00290556 Book/CD Pack $14.95

10. The Sound of Music
10 beloved songs from the musical: Climb Ev'ry Mountain • Do-Re-Mi • Edelweiss • The Lonely Goatherd • Maria • My Favorite Things • Sixteen Going on Seventeen • So Long, Farewell • Something Good • The Sound of Music.

00290557 Book/CD Pack $16.95

11. Disney Early Favorites
10 great Disney duets: Give a Little Whistle • Heigh-Ho • Hi-Diddle-Dee-Dee (An Actor's Life for Me) • I'm Wishing • I've Got No Strings • Some Day My Prince Will Come • When I See an Elephant Fly • When You Wish upon a Star • Whistle While You Work • Who's Afraid of the Big Bad Wolf?

00290558 Book/CD Pack $16.95

12. Disney Movie Songs
9 well-known songs: The Bare Necessities • Be Our Guest • Chim Chim Cher-ee • Circle of Life • Cruella De Vil • God Help the Outcasts • If I Never Knew You (Love Theme from Pocahontas) • Part of Your World • A Whole New World.

00290559 Book/CD Pack $16.95

13. Movie Hits
8 film favorites: Theme from E.T. (The Extra-Terrestrial) • Forrest Gump – Main Title (Feather Theme) • The Godfather (Love Theme) • The John Dunbar Theme • Moon River • Romeo and Juliet (Love Theme) • Theme from Schindler's List • Somewhere, My Love.

00290560 Book/CD Pack $14.95

14. Les Misérables
8 great songs from the musical: Bring Him Home • Castle on a Cloud • Do You Hear the People Sing? • A Heart Full of Love • I Dreamed a Dream • In My Life • On My Own • Stars.

00290561 Book/CD Pack $16.95

15. God Bless America® & Other Songs for a Better Nation
8 patriotic duets: America, the Beautiful • Anchors Aweigh • Battle Hymn of the Republic • Climb Ev'ry Mountain • God Bless America • God Bless the U.S.A. • This Is My Country • What a Wonderful World.

00290562 Book/CD Pack $14.95

16. Disney Classics
10 favorites: Alice in Wonderland • The Ballad of Davy Crockett • Beauty and the Beast • It's a Small World • Lavender Blue (Dilly Dilly) • Little April Shower • Mickey Mouse March • Once upon a Dream • Supercalifragilisticexpialidocious • Under the Sea.

00290563 Book/CD Pack $16.95

17. High School Musical
9 songs from the TV hit production: Bop to the Top • Breaking Free • Get'cha Head in the Game • I Can't Take My Eyes Off of You • Start of Something New • Stick to the Status Quo • We're All in This Together • What I've Been Looking For • When There Was Me and You.

00290564 Book/CD Pack $16.95

18. High School Musical 2
8 songs from the sequel: All for One • Everyday • Fabulous • Gotta Go My Own Way • I Don't Dance • What Time Is It • Work This Out • You Are the Music in Me.

00290565 Book/CD Pack $16.95

19. Pirates of the Caribbean
9 pieces: The Black Pearl • Brethren Court • He's a Pirate • Jack Sparrow • The Kraken • The Medallion Calls • One Day • Up Is Down • Wheel of Fortune.

00290566 Book/CD Pack $16.95

20. Wicked
8 selections from this Broadway hit: Dancing Through Life • Defying Gravity • For Good • I Couldn't Be Happier • I'm Not That Girl • Popular • What Is This Feeling? • The Wizard and I.

00290567 Book/CD Pack $16.95

21. Peanuts®
8 tunes from this animated classic: Blue Charlie Brown • Charlie Brown Theme • The Great Pumpkin Waltz • Joe Cool • Linus and Lucy • Oh, Good Grief • Red Baron • You're in Love, Charlie Brown.

00290568 Book/CD Pack $16.95

22. Rodgers & Hammerstein
10 songs from this dynamic duo: Do I Love You Because You're Beautiful? • Happy Talk • Hello, Young Lovers • I Whistle a Happy Tune • If I Loved You • My Favorite Things • People Will Say We're in Love • Some Enchanted Evening • The Surrey with the Fringe on Top • You'll Never Walk Alone.

00290569 Book/CD Pack $14.95

23. Cole Porter
10 tunes from the legendary composer: Another Op'nin', Another Show • Easy to Love (You'd Be So Easy to Love) • From This Moment On • I Love Paris • I Love You • I've Got You Under My Skin • In the Still of the Night • It's Delovely • So in Love • You'd Be So Nice to Come Home To.

00290570 Book/CD Pack $14.95

24. Christmas Carols
9 holiday favorites: Angels We Have Heard on High • Ding Dong! Merrily on High! • The First Noel • God Rest Ye Merry, Gentlemen • Hark! the Herald Angels Sing • It Came upon the Midnight Clear • O Come, All Ye Faithful (Adeste Fideles) • O Little Town of Bethlehem • What Child Is This?

00290571 Book/CD Pack $14.95

25. Wedding Songs
8 great songs for going down the aisle: Bless the Broken Road • From This Moment On • Grow Old with Me • Here and Now • I Will Be Here • Sunrise, Sunset • We've Only Just Begun • Wedding Song (There Is Love).

00290572 Book/CD Pack $14.95

26. Love Songs
8 tender songs from the heart: All I Ask of You • (Everything I Do) I Do It for You • Here, There and Everywhere • I Will Always Love You • Longer • Somewhere Out There • Up Where We Belong • Your Song.

00290573 Book/CD Pack $14.95

27. Romantic Favorites
8 songs of romance: Endless Love • Just the Way You Are • Romeo and Juliet (Love Theme) • Save the Best for Last • Till There Was You • Unchained Melody • Valentine • You Are the Sunshine of My Life.

00290574 Book/CD Pack $14.95

31. Pride and Prejudice
8 arrangements from the 2006 Oscar-nominated film: Another Dance • Arrival at Netherfield • Dawn • Georgiana • Leaving Netherfield • Meryton Townhall • Mrs. Darcy • The Secret Life of Daydreams.

00290578 Book/CD Pack $14.95